Applied Magic

A beginner's magic book with practical applications for therapists, teachers, and parents

Applied Magic

A beginner's magic book with
practical applications for
therapists, teachers, and parents

Michael Kett

Illustrated by Nancy Kett

Copyright © 2000 by Michael Kett.

Library of Congress Number: 00-192196
ISBN #:   Hardcover   0-7388-3825-X
               Softcover   0-7388-3826-8

This book was printed in the United States of America.

To order additional copies of this book, contact:
Xlibris Corporation
1-888-7-XLIBRIS
www.Xlibris.com
Orders@Xlibris.com

Contents

Acknowledgments

This book is dedicated to my dad, for kindling the spark of magic within me.

Applied Magic is a result of my more than 20 years as a physical therapist and a magician. Many people influenced me along the way. Jeff McBride shared with me his philosophy of blending one's passions with his magic. This book is a result of that philosophy. Joel Davenport, the other Houkali Wizard and lifelong friend, has always shared my passion for magic. His enthusiastic support and insights have been an inspiration to me. A number of professionals, Melinda Buehring, Peggy Stell, Lee Phelps, Colleen Lundell, Ann Swiderek, Chet Wolkowicz, and Tim Hannig, were kind enough to review this book and provide feedback. My son Bryan provided off-the-cuff ideas and comments that contributed to this book, as well as my ongoing development as a magician. My wife Nancy not only illustrated this book, but without her encouragement and love, this book would still only be a dream.

Introduction

Let me start by explaining what this book is not. It is not strictly a magic book with the end result of "fooling your friends and family." Rather, it's a book that applies magic to various fields, such as therapy, teaching, and public speaking. It is also an excellent beginner magic book for parents wishing to spend time interacting with their children.

In 1981, David Copperfield developed Project Magic, in conjunction with an occupational therapist. This program was designed to teach basic magic tricks to patients of occupational therapists. Over the years, I have come to realize that magic has many additional applications. Magic can also be used as a therapeutic tool to enhance motor and speaking skills in physical and speech therapy. Furthermore, teachers can incorporate magic into storytelling and directed motor activities, as well as encourage its use by students as a less intimidating means of public speaking. Performing magic builds self-confidence, whether it is in a classroom, in a clinic, or in front of an audience.

It is up to the individual therapist, teacher, parent, or activity director to choose the appropriate magic effect or activity from this book. To some degree, all the magic in this book addresses eye-hand coordination, motor planning, sequencing, gross or fine motor control, visual and auditory attention, creative thinking, and social interaction. The book is divided into five major sections: IceBreakers, Magic with A Purpose, Mind Bending Magic, Fantastic Fun, and Magic That Tells A Story.

Each magic effect has a difficulty rating. When appropriate, other variations are suggested. The difficulty level of each magic effect can be altered in a number of ways, such as changing postures or using the opposite hand. By combining two or three magic effects, a number of therapeutic goals can be achieved.

I purposely avoided including any card magic because I prefer to use everyday objects. I also purposely avoided using the term magic "trick" throughout the book. The word "trick" can establish a win/lose or puzzle attitude. It is my hope that both the performer and the spectator are viewed as equals.

The effects taught in this book can be found in various versions scattered among numerous beginner magic books. Some of the activities in this book may even be considered stunts or jokes. A number of therapists and magicians have helped review the specific magic effects and therapeutic considerations. Therefore, while this book can be used as a beginner magic book by anyone, what makes it unique is that it gives magic a purpose beyond basic entertainment.

1 | Basic Magic Principles

It is not only the secret that makes a trick appear to be magic. It is also the attention to detail, the story behind the effect and some basic principles of magic. There are many magic principles, but I feel these are the most important ones for a new magician.

Eye Power

One of the most basic magic principles is that "The audience will look where you look." If you pretend to put a coin in your left hand and you concentrate your gaze on the left hand, the audience will also look there. As an experiment the next time you are shopping, stop and stare at the ceiling. In a few seconds I bet you won't be the only person staring at the ceiling. Another application is looking into the spectator's eyes and asking a question. When the spectator looks up to answer, you can perform the "secret move."

Believe It!

For the audience to believe what you're doing is real, you have to believe it is real. If you pretend to put a coin in your left hand, you must believe that the coin is actually in your left hand. In your mind you must "feel" the coin actually in your left hand to be able to convey that to the audience.

Is It Natural?

Every movement you make must appear natural. Quick movements as in "the hand is quicker than the eye" are suspicious. The best way to test yourself is to actually perform the movement, such as putting a coin in your left hand. Watch yourself in a mirror. Next, pretend to put the coin in the left hand. Did it look the same as when you actually placed the coin in the left hand? If not, you need to practice until the two movements look the same.

Puzzle, Trick, or Magic?

Puzzles and tricks are not necessarily magic. If you present your magic as a puzzle or call it a trick, people will tend to feel challenged to figure out how the trick works. Why not call your tricks "magic effects" or "experiments"? I know it is a small point, but I think it makes a difference. If you can take a magic effect and relate it to a story, especially something that you have a passion about, the effect will become an opportunity to share a part of you with the audience rather than presenting a challenge or puzzle.

2 | How to Teach Magic

Teaching Sequence

One to one instruction is the ideal situation. In many instances, that may not be practical. Having students work in pairs provides them with peer feedback. This type of feedback not only provides social interaction, but allows the partners the opportunity to observe and make recommendations.

Before the students learn and practice each magic effect, you have to demonstrate it properly, hopefully, with some type of story or lesson. Once you have performed it, explain how the effect works. Break the effect down into component parts and teach each component separately. Gradually combine components into a sequence until the entire effect is learned. Of course, depending on the student and the difficulty of the effect, there will be various steps to teach. It may be helpful to have the student focus on developing a feel for the movement, rather than the actual mechanics. Too much attention on the mechanics can lead to "paralysis from analysis." Emphasize what "to do" rather than what "not to do" and use praise and encouragement frequently. When providing verbal cues, limit the cues to only a few words at a time.

Have each student perform the effect for his partner. This type of interaction may be less threatening when it is applied in a teaching rather than a performing situation. Learning some of these magic effects will improve the student's self-confidence. He will be able to accomplish things (magic) that other individuals cannot.

You may want to take time to develop a story for the effect with input from the entire group. Have each student practice telling the story as the effect is performed. Another suggestion would be to have each student develop her own story to present to the entire class.

Videotaping your student's performance is a tremendous tool. The entire group can learn from each individual student's performance. Each student can perform a different effect to create a complete show on video for parents, teachers and other students to enjoy.

Environment

For a group, a classroom situation with a table and chairs is ideal. The next option would be to have the students sit on the floor. Any room with minimal outside distractions is satisfactory.

Props

All the effects in this book can be accomplished with objects found around the house. Many of the effects don't require any props or special preparation. I purposely avoided card effects, but if you would like to teach some card magic, check out any of the books in the bibliography.

Practice

Unfortunately, much of the magic marketed today is advertised as "easy to do." It may be easy to do, but most likely will be performed very poorly. To allow new motor skills to become permanent, the magic effect needs to be practiced a little bit (five to ten minutes) frequently, over a period of days or weeks. Once the student can perform the mechanics of the effect perfectly, he can concentrate more on the story or presentation. Eventually, a series of two to three effects can be combined into a short routine.

Choosing the Correct Magic Effect

It would be impossible to make specific recommendations regarding which magic effect would be appropriate for every type of motor skill need or diagnosis. My recommendation is to try the effect or activity yourself to determine if it is appropriate. If the entire effect is too difficult, you may want to choose one or two of the component parts on which to concentrate initially. I wouldn't recommend teaching and practicing more than two or three effects at a time unless they were very different (i.e. combine a gross motor and a fine motor or mental effect).

Difficulty Level

The difficulty level of each magic effect can be altered in a number of ways, such as changing postures (sitting, standing, kneeling, standing on one leg), crossing the body's midline, using the opposite hand, watching oneself in a mirror, or concentrating on the story that accompanies the piece of magic. The difficulty of each effect is rated on a 1—3 star scale with 1 star signifying the least difficult. One or more of the characteristics listed under each category below may apply to a particular effect. All categories utilize sequencing, visual motor coordination and motor planning.

* Easy

- Utilizes gross motor skills
- Primarily uses dominant hand

- Involves symmetrical upper extremity movements
- Involves few steps
- Requires minimal verbal cueing
- Good beginner magic effect

** Challenging

- Utilizes some fine motor skills
- Uses both hands
- Involves asymmetrical upper extremity movements
- May require moderate verbal cueing
- Involves crossing the midline

*** Complex

- Utilizes significant degree of fine motor skill
- Consistently uses both hands
- Involves numerous steps requiring integration of concurrent bilateral motor activities
- May require significant verbal cueing

3 | Icebreakers

You have to get a person's attention before you can teach anything. The following ideas can help you capture an individual's or group's attention by creating laughter, surprise or amazement. You can tie in your attention getting technique with your topic to create a smooth transition. Try the following and use your imagination to create variations.

Squeaker *

You can purchase a squeaker at most novelty shops. It is plastic and about the size of a half-dollar and is easily concealed in the hand. Ideas include: squeeze your nose or someone else's nose, pat your head and mention that your hair is squeaky clean, squeak as you pick something up such as a pencil or book, have a child squeeze your nose as you squeak the squeaker, use it in conjunction with a stuffed animal or picture of an animal, squeak as you hop up and down or only squeak when you hop on one leg, or squeak as you clean your glasses with a cloth. There are hundreds of applications for this low-tech prop.

Watch Winder *

You can also purchase a watch winder at most novelty shops. It is a small metal wheel that creates a ratchety sound when it is turned. It is great for pretending to "wind something with an invisible key," opening a box or door, and bending your "creaky knee." It creates a unique auditory effect.

Judy the Mouse *

A "Judy the Mouse" can also be purchased at most novelty or magic shops. It is about the size of a real mouse. Your thumb fits inside to make it scurry up your body or eat out of your hand. In fact, you can use it in combination with a squeaker. Even though most people (those over about five years of age) know it isn't alive, it is a fantastic icebreaker.

Superman *

No props are needed for with this one. All you need is a doorway. The door must be opened. The opened doorway will be the frame for the people watching. Stand on one leg and bend at the hip as you lean forward to get your upper body parallel to the floor. Keep your arms overhead like you are flying (Figure 3-1). If you have enough balance and strength, bend and straighten the knee of the leg on which you are standing, to give the appearance of "changing altitude" as you fly. This is a great gag!

Figure 3-1

CLIMBING THE WALL *

You are using the doorway again for this one. Stand on one leg and use your arms to "pull yourself up" one of the door-jambs, as if you were trying to climb over a fence or wall (Figure 3-2). Really act as if you are having difficulty pulling yourself up; maybe even pretend to "slip" and barely catch yourself from falling. This one will take a little practice to look good, but it is definitely worth the effort.

Figure 3-2

Arm Twist *

This is an outstanding activity to use when discussing flexibility or as part of a "stand-up stretch break" during a presentation. Demonstrate at the same time that you have the audience follow these instructions:

Keep your arms in front of you with your elbows straight; rotate your arms so your thumbs are pointing at the floor.

Cross your arms so your palms are facing each other, then interlace your fingers together. While instructing your students to keep their elbows straight and fingers locked, ask them to rotate their arms so their thumbs point toward the ceiling. It is impossible, unless you cheat.

Here is how you cheat: after demonstrating the correct technique, unlock your arms and check one of the students to make sure her elbows are totally straight. When you resume the arm position to continue, you don't perform the technique as you taught it. You lace your fingers together with the thumbs up, then twist your arms to point the thumbs down. If done quickly and nonchalantly, it won't be noticed. At a glance, your arm position looks similar to that of the students. Slowly "untwist" your arms so the thumbs point to the ceiling while asking your students to do the same. They won't be able to do it if they keep their elbows straight and fingers laced together as instructed.

Vanishing Leg *

You need a jacket or towel for this effect. The only preparation is loosening your shoe on your left foot. Stand and place the jacket or towel in front of you so it covers you from the waist and extends to the floor. Carefully slip your foot out of the loose shoe by standing on the opposite foot. Bend the knee of the leg without the shoe so that your calf is parallel to the floor. Slowly raise the jacket or towel so it is just below knee level. It will look as if your leg has vanished and all that remains is your left shoe.

Reverse the process to have your leg reappear. Obviously, you need to have good balance standing on one leg.

Finger Palm Vanish **

The finger palm vanish can be used to vanish any small object. Start by displaying a coin in your right hand at the base of the middle and ring fingers. Your left hand is palm up just below the right hand (Figure 3-3a). Your right hand turns palm down to apparently drop the coin into the left hand. As you do this, the right fingers curl a little, just enough to keep the coin from falling out of the hand (Figure 3-3b). This is the finger palm position. At the same time, your left hand closes into a fist as if it has just received the coin. Look at the left hand (which supposedly contains the coin), as you casually drop your right hand to your side. Slowly open your left hand to show that the coin has vanished. Practice this in front of a mirror by actually placing the coin in the left hand. The finger palm should look exactly the same as actually placing the coin in the left hand.

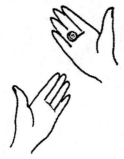

Figure 3-3a   Figure 3-3b

Basic Production *

Once you have vanished an object using the finger palm technique, you can reproduce the object from virtually anywhere—from behind someone's ear, the back of your elbow or knee, your pocket, etc. Make the object appear at your finger tips rather than the palm of your hand, by moving the object to your fingertips before it is reproduced.

4 | Magic With A Purpose

Gross Motor Control Magic Effects

On the whole, the gross motor skill effects are the easiest. I'd recommend starting with one or two gross motor control effects to build the student's confidence. Of course, the actual effect you choose will depend on specific motor skill goals, as well as the student's age and ability.

Vanishing Leg *

Refer to Chapter 3 (Icebreakers) for the explanation.

THERAPEUTIC CONSIDERATIONS: This effect can be performed in a doorway for students that have difficulty balancing on one leg. The student can use the doorway for arm support as needed, or just lean against one side of the doorjamb. Have the student try it with both legs (but not at the same time!).

Arm Twist *

Refer to Chapter 3 (Icebreakers) for the explanation.

TEACHING TIPS: Practice the "secret move" so it doesn't look suspicious. If you continue talking while performing the move, no one will notice.

THERAPEUTIC CONSIDERATIONS: This effect is a good basic activity for crossing the midline and bilateral coordination. It requires good shoulder internal rotation. You may want to incorporate this into a warm-up routine after performing a number of normal stretches.

Rubber Quarter *

WHAT THE AUDIENCE SEES: The performer is able to bend a quarter, half dollar, or any other flat solid object that she can hold in her hand.

PROPS/SPECIAL PREPARATION: a quarter, half-dollar, or silver dollar.

ROUTINE:

The secret is in the wrist action. Hold the coin vertically at chest level with both hands.

Keep the index and middle fingers in front and the thumbs behind the coin. Bend your wrists toward you (flexion) so the coin moves toward your body as your elbows come slightly away from your body. Then, bend your wrists back (extension) as your elbows move back toward your body. It will create the illusion that the coin is bending back and forth.

TEACHING TIPS: Practice this in front of a mirror to get the feel of how far to bend your wrists and move your elbows to achieve the optimum effect.

THERAPEUTIC CONSIDERATIONS: This is a good wrist activity requiring symmetrical upper extremity movement. Pincer grip is also utilized.

Penny Attraction *

WHAT THE AUDIENCE SEES: The performer rubs a penny between her hands to make it "magical." She then places the penny on top of her head and puts one hand palm down on top of the penny. A spectator is invited to try to lift the performer's hand off the penny but is unable to do so.

PROPS/SPECIAL PREPARATION: Any coin will work.

ROUTINE:

There really is no secret to this effect. The performer has a significant strength advantage in this position. No matter how hard the spectator tries, he is unable to lift the performer's hand off the coin.

TEACHING TIPS: Make sure the instructions are to lift the performer's hand straight up at the wrist off her head, rather than sliding it.

THERAPEUTIC CONSIDERATIONS: This is a good balance and trunk stabilization exercise, which also involves upper extremity strength and mobility. It can be performed with both hands simultaneously or in various developmental postures.

Quick Knot *

WHAT THE AUDIENCE SEES: A knot is tied in a piece of rope without letting go of the ends.

PROPS/SPECIAL PREPARATION: A piece of rope 36 inches long.

ROUTINE:

Hold one end of the rope in the web space of your left hand, and drape the other end over the right hand as shown in Figure 4-1a.

As you bring both hands together, pinch point A between the index and middle fingers of the right hand. At the same time, pinch point B between the index and middle fingers of left hand (Figure 4-1b).

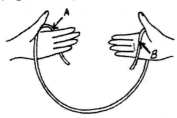

Figure 4-1a

Figure 4-1b

Move your hands apart and a knot will form in the center of the rope (Figure 4-1c).

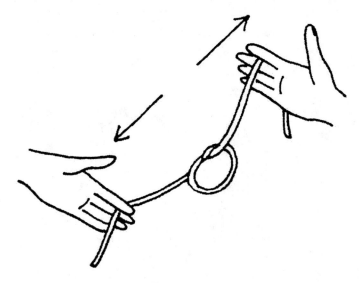

Figure 4-1c

Teaching tips: To make this more amazing, practice until you can perform it very quickly.

Therapeutic considerations: This is an excellent effect for motor planning and bilateral coordination. Work toward having the student not look at his hands while forming the knot. Try combining this and a few of the following rope effects into a short routine of rope magic.

Instant Knot *

What the audience sees: The performer asks a volunteer to tie a knot in a piece of rope without letting go of the ends. When the volunteer is unable to do so, the performer demonstrates how it can be accomplished.

Props/special preparation: A piece of rope 30-36 inches long.

Routine:

Cross your arms as in Figure 4-2a. Grasp an end of the rope in each hand.

Slowly uncross your arms and the knot will appear (Figure 4-2b).

Figure 4-2a   Figure 4-2b

TEACHING TIPS: Try to get agreement from the audience that it is impossible to tie a knot in the rope without letting go of the ends before you demonstrate the technique.

THERAPEUTIC CONSIDERATIONS: If the student is unable to grasp the rope while his arms are crossed, have someone place the rope in his hands.

Snap Knot *

WHAT THE AUDIENCE SEES: The performer holds a rope in one hand. The performer attempts to snap the rope to form a knot in it. On the third attempt, a knot appears at the end of the rope.

PROPS/SPECIAL PREPARATION: A piece of rope 24 inches long. Prior to performing, tie a knot about three inches from one of the ends.

ROUTINE:

Hold the rope between the right thumb and index finger, keeping the knot hidden in the palm of the hand.

With the left hand, bring the end of the rope without the knot up to your right hand, and hold it between the right index and middle fingers.

Snap the wrist down as you release the end without the knot.

Repeat again. The third time, release the end with the knot to make the knot magically appear.

TEACHING TIPS: This is a good beginning effect to increase self-confidence.

THERAPEUTIC CONSIDERATIONS: The student can start with the rope in the left hand (keeping the knot hidden in the palm), then pass the rope to the right hand before performing the effect, to utilize both hands. He may perform this effect in the opposite hand to increase difficulty. Have the student perform this effect at multiple angles of shoulder elevation (flexion or abduction) to facilitate scapular stabilization.

Anti-gravity Pencil #1 *

WHAT THE AUDIENCE SEES: The performer holds a pen or pencil in his left fist. As he opens his fingers one by one, the pencil remains in his hand as if defying gravity.

PROPS/SPECIAL PREPARATION: A pen, pencil, or similar object.

ROUTINE:

Rub the pen along your sleeve to develop a "static electric charge." Hold your left palm up, and lay the pen in it. Close your hand around the pen. Turn your hand so the back of the hand faces the audience.

Grasp your left wrist with your right hand, keeping your right index finger straight. Your left wrist hides the right index finger. Put the tip of the right index finger against the pen inside your left fist.

Slowly straighten each finger of the left hand. The pen will remain against the left palm, thanks to the help of your right index finger.

Slowly make a fist again with your left hand and remove the right hand from around the wrist. Figure 4-3a shows the secret behind the effect. Figure 4-3b shows the audience's view.

Figure 4-3a   Figure 4-3b

TEACHING TIPS: Make a real show of creating the static electric charge and open your left hand very slowly to build the suspense. Be sure to angle your left hand down, so the audience sees only the back of your left hand.

THERAPEUTIC CONSIDERATIONS: You can have the student raise his hand overhead or across his body while the pen is suspended, to work range of motion or crossing the midline activities.

Anti-gravity Pencil #2 **

WHAT THE AUDIENCE SEES: The performer holds a pen in his folded hands with fingers interlaced. As he slowly brings his palms apart, keeping the fingers interlaced, the pen remains against his hand as if defying gravity.

PROPS/SPECIAL PREPARATION: A pen, pencil or similar object.

ROUTINE:

This effect is more difficult than the previous version. Once again rub the pen along your sleeve to create a "static electric charge." Hold the pen in the left hand.

Maintain control of the pen with your thumb, as the right hand comes across to lace the fingers together. The secret is that the right middle finger does not lace with the left fingers. This finger is secretly free in the palm to hold the pen against the other fingers (Figure 4-4).

Pretend to hold the top of the pen with both thumbs. Slowly remove the thumbs so that they are not touching the pen. It looks as if the pen is defying gravity.

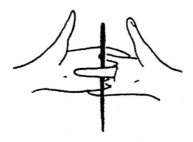

Figure 4-4

TEACHING TIPS: Make sure that both the top and bottom of the pen are visible above and below the hands. To make interlacing the fingers look natural, practice interlacing them as above without the pen first, then practice with the pen.

THERAPEUTIC CONSIDERATIONS: Gradually increase the speed of lacing the fingers together to increase the difficulty. Also, have the student use different fingers to secretly hold the pen against the other fingers.

Vanishing Pen and Quarter **

WHAT THE AUDIENCE SEES: Performer displays a quarter to the audience. He tells them he is going to make the quarter vanish. He taps the quarter with a pencil three times, but the pencil disappears instead. He apologizes for the mistake and discovers the pencil behind his ear. Once again he tries to make the coin disappear by tapping it with the pencil three times. This time the coin has disappeared.

PROPS/SPECIAL PREPARATION: A pencil or pen and a quarter.

ROUTINE:

Show the quarter on the palm of your left hand. Keep the hand at waist level and turn your body's left side toward the audience. Tell the audience that you will make the quarter vanish.

Tap the quarter three times with the pencil as you count "one, two, and three," but before each tap raise the pencil to the level of your right ear. Before the third count, secretly place the pencil behind your right ear and bring the empty right hand down and slap it against the quarter. Don't worry, no one will see that you put the pencil behind your ear because they are looking at the quarter.

Admit that you made a mistake and made the pencil disappear. Turn your entire body to the left and point with your right hand to the pencil behind your ear. Make a joke of the fact that you put the pencil behind your ear.

As everyone is looking at the pencil behind your right ear, drop the quarter from your left hand into your left pants pocket, then close your hand. Tell the audience you will try it again.

This time, count and tap your closed fist with the pencil. Open your hand to show that this time the quarter has really vanished.

TEACHING TIPS: This effect works entirely by directing the audience's attention. It is a great application of timing and focusing the audience's attention away from the secret move.

THERAPEUTIC CONSIDERATIONS: Crossing the midline is key to this effect. This effect can be used to facilitate standing balance. It can also be performed sitting, for individuals with impaired standing balance. If the student has difficulty with trunk rotation, he may perform this effect seated on a swivel chair.

Ring off String **

WHAT THE AUDIENCE SEES: Performer borrows a finger ring and threads it onto a piece of string. Two spectators each hold one of the ends of the string. The performer rubs his hands together and the ring penetrates the string.

PROPS/SPECIAL PREPARATION: A finger ring and a 30-inch piece of string.

ROUTINE:
Have a spectator thread the ring onto the string. Display the ring on the center of the string on the palm of your left hand

(Figure 4-5a). It is helpful if the ring is more toward the little finger side of the palm.

Close your left hand and turn it over so the back of the hand is facing up (Figure 4-5b).

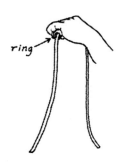

Figure 4-5a   Figure 4-5b

With your right hand, grasp the string where it comes out of the left fist on the thumb side, and slide your right hand along the string and give the end to a spectator (Figure 4-5c).

Look the spectator in the eye and say "Hold on tightly to this end." Now reach your right hand across the top of the left fist and grasp the string as it comes out the little finger side of the left hand.

At this point slightly tilt your left hand, so the ring will slide out of your left hand and into the cupped fingers of the right hand as it is grasping the string (Figure 4-5d). Continue sliding your right hand along the string.

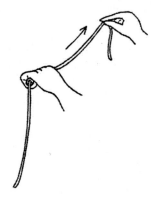

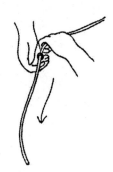

Figure 4-5c   Figure 4-5d

The ring will secretly slide off the string. Once your right hand reaches the end of the string, hand another spectator that end.

At this point look the spectator in the eye and say "Hold on tightly to this end." This will take the spectator's attention away from your right hand, which is secretly holding the ring.

Move your right hand palm down to below the left hand that is holding the string. Twist your right hand palm up and place your hands together (Figure 4-5e).

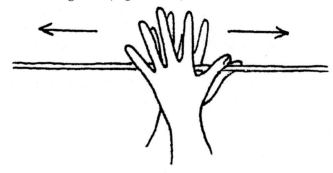

Figure 4-5e

Instruct the spectators to pull the ends of the string, keeping it taught.

Slide your hands together back and forth along the string. Lift your left hand to show that the ring has penetrated the string.

TEACHING TIPS: You could also use a small washer rather than a finger ring.

THERAPEUTIC CONSIDERATIONS: This effect requires adequate pronation and supination of both forearms.

Jumping Dime ***

WHAT THE AUDIENCE SEES: The performer displays a dime at the right fingertips. Both hands are slapped against the stomach. The dime is now shown to be in the left hand.

PROPS/SPECIAL PREPARATION: Only one dime is used.

ROUTINE:

With palm up, place the dime on the fingertips of your right hand.

Display both hands palm up, at waist level. Both hands are slapped against the stomach at the same time.

The fingertips of the hands are about three to four inches apart when the hands are against the stomach.

The dime is transferred to the opposite hand as your hands are slapped against your body. The dime is actually trapped between your stomach and opposite hand. No one will see the dime travel from one hand to the other.

Keeping your left hand against your stomach, show that your right hand is now empty. Then show that the dime has "jumped" to your left hand.

TEACHING TIPS: Try doing this at various speeds in front of a mirror to learn the correct technique.

THERAPEUTIC CONSIDERATIONS: Progress by starting to use a larger coin before using a dime. Once the effect is mastered using the dominant hand, have the student try it with the coin starting in the nondominant hand.

5 | More Magic With A Purpose

Fine Motor Control Magic Effects

CUT AND RESTORED STRING *

WHAT THE AUDIENCE SEES: Performer displays a plastic straw and a 12-inch piece of string. The string is threaded through the straw and the straw is bent in half. The straw and string are cut at the bend in the straw. The two ends of the straw are shown actually cut. The performer places the cut ends of the straw together and pulls the string out unharmed.

PROPS/SPECIAL PREPARATION: A plastic straw, a 12-inch piece of string, and scissors. With the scissors or an exacto-knife, cut a two-inch lengthwise slit in the center of the straw.

ROUTINE:

Display the string and straw, being careful not to let the audience see the slit in the straw.

Thread the string through the straw and demonstrate that it can be pulled freely through the straw.

Fold the straw in half, being careful to bend the straw so the secret slit is on the "inside" of the bend.

Pull both ends of the string down and the string will be pulled down into the secret slit (Figure 5-1a).

Cut the straw at the bend (Figure 5-1b).

Display both halves of the straw, but keep the two half pieces of the straw side by side.

To restore the string, place the two cut ends of the straw together and pull out the undamaged string.

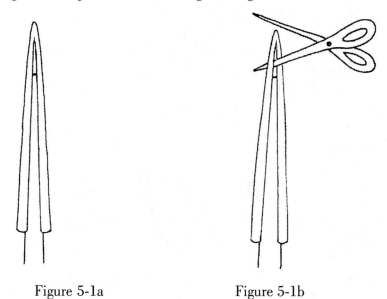

Figure 5-1a   Figure 5-1b

TEACHING TIPS: I'd recommend pre-cutting the slit in the straw for young children. Straws with stripes will hide the slit more effectively than a solid color straw.

THERAPEUTIC CONSIDERATIONS: This effect can be a sequel to another magic effect in this chapter, String Fusion, to create a short routine.

Coin Vanishing Handkerchief *

WHAT THE AUDIENCE SEES: Performer displays a coin and handkerchief. A member of the audience places the coin in the middle of the handkerchief. The performer grasps one corner of the handkerchief and shakes it to show that the coin has vanished.

PROPS/SPECIAL PREPARATION: A quarter, a small rubber band,

and a handkerchief. Place the rubber band around the thumb, index, and middle fingers of the left hand. Don't let the audience know about the rubber band.

ROUTINE:

Place the handkerchief over the left hand with the middle of it directly over the fingers with the rubber band.

Spread the left fingers apart to make a larger circle with the rubber band.

Use the right index finger to make a small pocket in the center of the handkerchief and poke the handkerchief below the rubber band.

Allow a member of the audience to drop the coin into the center of the handkerchief.

Let the rubber band slip off your left fingers and it will close around the coin.

Grasp one corner of the handkerchief with the right hand and shake it to show that the coin has vanished.

TEACHING TIPS: If you can't find a small enough rubber band, use a larger one and double it to create one with a smaller diameter. A colored or more opaque handkerchief will hide the rubber band more effectively.

THERAPEUTIC CONSIDERATIONS: This is a good beginner effect.

Jumping Rubber Band *

WHAT THE AUDIENCE SEES: The performer places a rubber band around his index and middle fingers. He closes his hand into a fist, and when he opens his hand the rubber band jumps to his ring and little fingers.

PROPS/SPECIAL PREPARATION: A small colored rubber band works best.

ROUTINE:

Put the rubber band around your left index and middle fingers (Figure 5-2a).

Show both sides of your hand to the audience. With your

palm facing you, close your hand into a fist. As you close your left hand into a fist, secretly hook the bottom end of the rubber band with your right index finger and pull it down toward your wrist (Figure 5-2b).

Figure 5-2a   Figure 5-2b

As you do this place the fingertips of all your left fingers inside this loop (Figure 5-2c). Don't let the audience see you do this.

Figure 5-2c

Now straighten your fingers and the rubber band will jump to your ring and little fingers.

TEACHING TIPS: Practice this with both hands. You can have the rubber band return back to the index and middle fingers by performing the same secret move of pulling the rubber band down and placing all your finger tips into the loop.

THERAPEUTIC CONSIDERATIONS: Using stronger rubber bands will increase finger strength. To perform the effect one handed, the student may use the thumb to create the secret loop rather than the index finger of the opposite hand.

Linking Paper Clips *

WHAT THE AUDIENCE SEES: The performer places two paper clips several inches apart on a folded dollar bill. The ends of the dollar bill are pulled apart. The paper clips jump from the bill and are magically linked together.

PROPS/SPECIAL PREPARATION: Two paper clips and a real (or play) dollar bill.

ROUTINE:

This effect actually works itself.

Fold one third of the dollar bill from left to right and put a paper clip over the number 1 on the bill (Figure 5-3a).

Now turn the bill completely around keeping the paper clip on top. Fold the left one-third of the bill over (Figure 5-3b).

Figure 5-3a   Figure 5-3b

Put the second paper clip over the right top edge, but make sure you only place it on the two layers closest to you. (Figure 5-3c). Once again, place this clip over the number 1 on the bill.

Figure 5-3c

Grasp the bill at each of the top corners and slowly pull. The clips will start to move toward each other.

When they are almost touching, pull the ends of the bill apart more quickly and the paper clips will link and jump off the bill.

TEACHING TIPS: To further simplify things, you may also want to put a small "x" on the top of the bill where each of the folds should take place.

THERAPEUTIC CONSIDERATIONS: This effect can be made easier by using larger paper clips or possibly a jumbo bill (or at least a larger piece of paper).

Linking Paper Clips and Rubber Band *

WHAT THE AUDIENCE SEES: The performer clips two paper clips to a folded dollar bill, and also places a rubber band around it. The ends of the dollar bill are pulled apart and the paper clips are found to be linked together, as well as onto the rubber band.

PROPS/SPECIAL PREPARATION: Two paper clips, a rubber band that can loosely fit around a dollar bill, and a real (or play) dollar bill.

ROUTINE:

Exactly as previous effect, except that you loop a rubber band around the bill after you place the first paper clip on the bill (Figure 5-4). After pulling the ends of the bill apart, the paper clips are linked to each other, as well as to the rubber band.

Figure 5-4

TEACHING TIPS: Have the student master the effect without using the rubber band before attempting this version.

Topsy Turvey Bill *

WHAT THE AUDIENCE SEES: Performer slowly folds a right side up dollar bill four times. When the bill is unfolded, it is upside down.

PROPS/SPECIAL PREPARATION: A real or play money dollar bill.

ROUTINE:

Hold the bill right side up with the picture of the president facing the audience. All the folds will fold the bill in half by moving the bill away from you.

Fold the bill in half from left to right.

Fold it in half again by folding the top half down toward the bottom.

Fold it a third time from left to right again.

Folding the top half down toward the bottom half again makes the last fold.

Now unfold the bill by first bringing up the bottom edge facing you. (If you first unfold the bill away from yourself the bill will not be upside down.)

TEACHING TIPS: You may want to prefold the bill until the student learns the folding process. It is very important to fold and unfold the bill slowly so that the audience doesn't suspect any "trickery."

THERAPEUTIC CONSIDERATIONS: This effect may be used to enhance thumb opposition and pinch grip.

Finger Palm Vanish *

WHAT THE AUDIENCE SEES: Performer displays a small coin or object in her right hand. The coin is placed in the other hand, as she gets out a pencil to use as a magic wand. The wand is waved over the left hand. The left hand is opened to show that the coin has vanished.

PROPS/SPECIAL PREPARATION: A coin or small object and a pencil.
ROUTINE:

This routine is almost identical to the Finger Palm Vanish described in Chapter 3 (IceBreakers).

Display a coin in your right hand at the base of the middle and index fingers (Figure 5-5a). Your left hand is palm up just below the right hand.

Say that you need your magic pencil and pretend to place the coin in your left hand. As you pretend to put the coin in the left hand, curl your right fingers slightly to keep the coin from falling out of the right hand (Figure 5-5b).

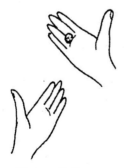

Figure 5-5a

Figure 5-5b

Close your left hand as if it has received the coin.

As you look at the left hand, reach into your right pocket to get a pencil, leave the coin in the pocket, and bring out the pencil.

Now use the pencil to wave over the left hand and show that the coin has vanished.

TEACHING TIPS: Practice really putting the coin in the left hand in front of a mirror. It should look the same way when you pretend to put the coin in the left hand. It is very important that the right hand look relaxed even though it is concealing the coin. Delaying the revelation that the coin has disappeared will make this more amazing.

THERAPEUTIC CONSIDERATIONS: An easier method to accomplish the secret move would be to use the tip of the right thumb to keep the coin in the right hand as it turns over, rather than curling the right fingers.

Loop the Loop *

WHAT THE AUDIENCE SEES: Performer displays two cloth loops. They are placed over her thumb. They not only change places, but one of the loops appears to penetrate the thumb completely.

PROPS/SPECIAL PREPARATION: Two different colored cloth craft loops used to make potholders, etc. A bag of 200 loops costs about $2.50 at any craft store.

ROUTINE:

Pass one loop through the other. Hold the top loop horizontally, between the right and left hands while the second loop hangs down vertically (Figure 5-6a).

Bring the ends of the horizontal loop together and place them over the left thumb (Figure 5-6b).

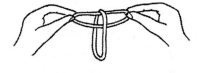 

Figure 5-6a   Figure 5-6b

Pinch the left index finger and thumb to create a closed circle. Pull a portion of the top loop down and it will change places with the bottom loop. (This is why it helps to have loops of different colors.)

Now take the bottom edge of the bottom loop and place it on the left thumb between the other loop and the end of the thumb (Figure 5-6c). Pinch the left index finger to the thumb again.

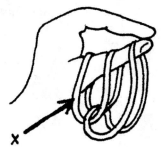

Figure 5-6c

Grasp the piece of loop nearest to the base of the thumb at point X and pull it down. It will appear to penetrate the thumb completely.

TEACHING TIPS: Make sure the thumb and index finger are not pinching the loops.

THERAPEUTIC CONSIDERATIONS: This is an excellent visual effect that is easy to do. It is also a good confidence builder.

Pinch Vanish **

WHAT THE AUDIENCE SEES: Performer displays a coin between her right thumb and index finger. She places it into her left hand, then reaches into her pocket to get a pencil. She taps the left fist with the pencil and opens her hand to show that the coin has vanished.

PROPS/SPECIAL PREPARATION: A coin and a pencil.

ROUTINE:

Display a coin between the thumb and index finger of the right hand (Figure 5-7a).

Hold your left hand at waist level, palm up below your right hand with the fingers slightly curled.

As you pretend to place the coin in the left hand, you perform the vanish. To accomplish the vanish, move your thumb and index fingers together to flatten the coin (Figure 5-7b).

Figure 5-7a   Figure 5-7b

Close your left hand as if it has received the coin.

Reach your right hand into your pocket to get a pencil and leave the coin there.

Tap the left fist with the pencil. Open the left hand to show that the coin has vanished.

TEACHING TIPS: A dime is probably the ideal size coin to use with most students. A quarter will work effectively with adults.

THERAPEUTIC CONSIDERATIONS: To increase the difficulty level, the student should not reach the right hand into the pocket to ditch the coin. Instead, she should keep the coin in the right hand after the vanish and transfer it to the curled ring and little fingers. She can then use her right thumb and middle finger to snap her fingers over the left fist. Then she can open her left fist to show that the coin has vanished. It will take some practice snapping the fingers while keeping the coin concealed in the same hand, but this will give the impression that there's nothing in the hand.

Afghan Bands **

WHAT THE AUDIENCE SEES: Three different colored paper loops are displayed. The performer cuts the first loop lengthwise and creates two separate loops of equal size. The second loop is cut lengthwise and creates two loops linked together. When the third loop is cut lengthwise, it forms one large loop.

PROPS/SPECIAL PREPARATION: Glue, scissors, colored paper. Cut strips of the paper three inches wide and glue them together to create three different colored strips of paper, each about 30 inches long. Gluing the ends together without twisting the paper (Figure 5-8a) makes the first loop. To make the second loop, one end is twisted 360 degrees before gluing the ends together (Figure 5-8b). The third loop is made by twisting one end 180 degrees before gluing the ends together (Figure 5-8c).

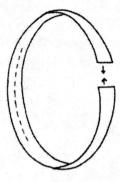

Figure 5-8a

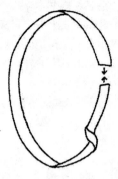

Figure 5-8b

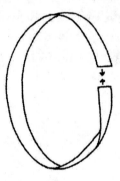

Figure 5-8c

ROUTINE:

Once the preparation is complete, this effect is self-working. Cut each entire loop lengthwise, as indicated by the dotted line in Figure 5-8a.

When you cut the loop that wasn't twisted, you will finish with two separate loops.

When you cut the loop that was twisted 360 degrees, you will finish with two loops linked together.

The loop with a 180-degree twist will produce one large loop.

TEACHING TIPS: You may want to have three different students all cut a different loop at the same time to finish with a different result. This will reduce the amount of time it would take for one student to cut all three loops. A good story will make this effect very entertaining (three children that are each unique—each cutting a different colored paper loop- resulting in three different loops).

THERAPEUTIC CONSIDERATIONS: This is an outstanding group activity. In addition to the actual effect, the preparation tasks can be used therapeutically to enhance visual coordination and prehension skills.

STRING FUSION **

WHAT THE AUDIENCE SEES: Two pieces of string are shown. A volunteer is asked to hold one end of each string. The performer covers the remaining two ends with one hand, and magically they fuse together to form a single piece of string.

PROPS/SPECIAL PREPARATION: You must use white cotton string for this effect. Cut off a piece of string about two feet long. At approximately the middle of the string, pull apart the strands of string with your fingernails, forming two one-inch long loops (Figure 5-9a). It is best if you can grasp about the same number of strands to make each loop. Retwist these loops in the direction they seem to want to twist. Twist and pull on the loops until they look like the ends of a string. By covering the junction of these loops with your thumb and index fingers, it will look like you have two separate pieces of string, rather than one long piece.

ROUTINE:

Casually display the 'two" pieces of string by holding the joint between your fingers (Figure 5-9b).

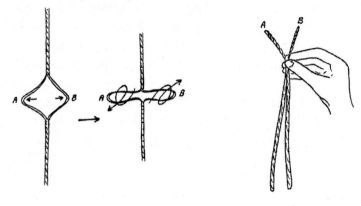

Figure 5-9a   Figure 5-9b

Hand someone one of the genuine ends of the string to hold. Hand another person the other genuine end.

Cover the other "two ends" (A and B) with one of your fists.

Slowly rub your fist along the center of the string. Make sure the spectators pull tightly on the string. If they aren't pulling the string tightly enough, you should pull the string toward yourself to create more tension in the string. It is the tension that helps restore the string.

Slowly open your hand to show the string restored.

TEACHING TIPS: You can use one spectator to hold a genuine end of the string in each hand, rather than involve two spectators.

THERAPEUTIC CONSIDERATIONS: It may be easier to separate the strands of the string with a toothpick, rather than fingernails.

DISSOLVING HANDKERCHIEF KNOT **

WHAT THE AUDIENCE SEES: Performer ties a knot in a handkerchief. A spectator blows on the handkerchief and the knot dissolves.

PROPS/SPECIAL PREPARATION: A handkerchief.

ROUTINE:

Grasp the diagonal corners of a handkerchief between the thumb and index fingers of each hand. Twirl the handkerchief to make it more streamlined (Figure 5-10a).

Hold the left end of the handkerchief in the web space of the left thumb and index finger.

Bring end B over to the left and hold it between the left thumb and index finger (Figure 5-10b).

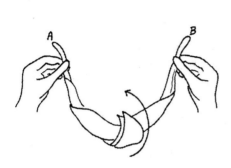

Figure 5-10a   Figure 5-10b

Reach through the loop with your right hand and grasp end B.

Pull end B over your left thumb and back through the loop toward you (Figure 5-10c). Keep your left thumb straight as you do this.

Continue pulling end B through the loop so it tightens around the left thumb. You now have what appears to be a knot.

Slide the thumb out of the loop of handkerchief and transfer the "knot" to the right hand, making sure to keep the "knot" from unfolding prematurely by holding it between the right thumb and index and middle fingers (Figure 5-10d).

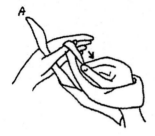

Figure 5-10c   Figure 5-10d

Have someone blow on the knot as you release pressure from the right thumb, gently snap your wrist, and the knot will appear to dissolve.

TEACHING TIPS: Practice making the "knot" without looking at your hands, so it will appear to be natural.

THERAPEUTIC CONSIDERATIONS: This may be difficult for students with small hands.

ONE HANDED KNOT ***

WHAT THE AUDIENCE SEES: A piece of rope is draped over the performer's hand. With a flick of the wrist, a knot appears in the rope.

PROPS/SPECIAL PREPARATION: A piece of rope 36 inches long.

ROUTINE:

Drape the rope over your right hand with one end between the ring and little fingers and the other end between your thumb and index finger (Figure 5-11a). The end of the rope hanging down from the little finger side of the hand extends a few inches lower than the other end.

Turning your hand palm down, grasp end "a" between the index and middle fingers at point B (Figure 5-11b).

Turn your hand back to the starting position, maintaining your grip on point B as you allow the loop that has formed around your hand to fall off your hand (Figure 5-11c). This loop will form a knot.

Figure 5-11a

Figure 5-11b

Figure 5-11c

TEACHING TIPS: After mastering the technique, try snapping the rope as the loop slides off your hand. It will look as if the knot magically appeared in the rope.

THERAPEUTIC CONSIDERATIONS: This effect should be practiced in small parts first. Step 5-11b should be practiced in slow motion because it is the most difficult part of the effect. The speed of 5-11c should be gradually increased to make the knot appear more quickly. As a variation, the student may try it with the opposite hand.

Coin Fold ***

WHAT THE AUDIENCE SEES: The performer has a coin marked by a spectator. The marked coin is folded inside a piece of paper. The paper is tapped on a table to prove that the coin is still in the folded paper. The performer tears the paper into pieces to show that the coin has vanished. The marked coin is then reproduced elsewhere.

PROPS/SPECIAL PREPARATION: A quarter or half dollar coin, a permanent marking pen, and a four inch square piece of paper.

ROUTINE:

Borrow a coin and have it marked with a marking pen. Display the piece of paper. With the left thumb and middle finger, hold the quarter in the center of the piece of paper.

With the right fingers fold the top half of the paper down toward you, making sure to completely cover the coin (Figure 5-12a). Note that this is not a symmetrical fold, but that the top edge stops short of the bottom edge by about one inch.

Next, fold the right half of the paper away from you. This secures the coin in the paper on the right side. Try not to make this fold exactly at the right edge of the coin. Leave about a quarter of an inch between this fold and the edge of the coin (Figure 5-12b).

Figure 5-12a   Figure 5-12b

Now fold the left side of the paper away from you. This secures the coin in the paper on the left side. Once again, leave about a quarter of an inch between the left edge of the coin and the fold (Figure 5-12c).

At this point, the coin is secured in the paper on all sides except the bottom edge.

Folding the bottom inch away from you (Figure 5-12d) makes the last fold. It will look to the audience as if the coin is secured in the paper on all four sides, but there is a secret opening in the bottom of the paper, facing you.

Figure 5-12c   Figure 5-12d

After you have made the last fold, squeeze firmly on the coin to create an impression of the coin in the paper.

Tap the folded paper on a table to prove that the coin is really there.

To make the coin vanish, hold the folded paper at your right finger tips with the secret opening of the paper pointed down into your palm. Relax the pressure in your thumb and fingers and the coin will slide out of the paper and into your hand.

After the coin is hidden in your right hand, take the folded paper in your left hand. Show both sides of the paper. The impression of the coin will convince the audience that the coin is still in the folded paper.

As you show the paper with your left hand, casually place your right hand into your pants pocket and leave the marked coin.

Use both hands to tear the paper and show that the coin has vanished. You can produce the coin from your pocket or finger palm it and produce it from a spectator's ear, etc.

TEACHING TIPS: This is a very amazing effect. The key is to make the folds slowly and deliberately. Gently squeezing the sides of the folded paper will help the coin to fall into your palm. Make sure to take some time between showing the folded paper with the coin in it and actually tearing it up to show that it has vanished.

THERAPEUTIC CONSIDERATIONS: The difficulty in this effect is that these small folds require precise dexterity.

Shoelace Knot ***

WHAT THE AUDIENCE SEES: A piece of rope is tied into a bow. The ends of the rope are put through the two loops of the bow. As the rope is pulled, a large knot develops. The performer wraps a hand around the knot, then slowly slides the knot off the rope. When he opens his hand, the knot has vanished.

PROPS/SPECIAL PREPARATION: A piece of rope 30 inches long.

ROUTINE:

Display the rope by holding it draped over the palms of the left and right hands. Keep the right hand below the left hand (Figure 5-13a).

Pinch the rope between the thumb and index finger of each hand, as the right hand moves up so it is even with the left hand (Figure 5-13b).

 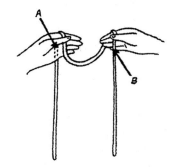

Figure 5-13a   Figure 5-13b

Pinch point A between the index and middle fingers of the right hand, as you pinch point B between the index and middle fingers of the left hand (Figure 5-13c).

Holding points A and B between your index and middle fingers of each hand, slowly move your hands apart to create a bowknot (Figure 5-13d). Pull the bowknot taut.

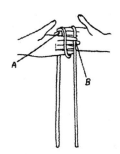 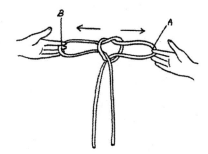

Figure 5-13c   Figure 5-13d

With your left thumb and index finger, reach through the left bow loop, pinch the left end of the rope, and pull it back toward you through the left bow loop (Figure 5-13e). Similarly, with your right thumb and index finger, reach through the right bow loop, pinch the right end of the rope, and pull it back toward you through the right bow loop.

Gently pull the ends of the rope apart to create the "knot" (Figure 5-13f). Don't pull too hard, or the knot will dissolve prematurely.

 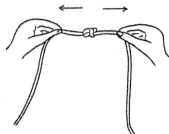

Figure 5-13e   Figure 5-13f

To make the knot vanish, you can pull quickly on the ends of the rope, or better yet, cover the knot with your hand and appear to slide the knot off the end of the rope. Actually, you work the knot free under cover of your hand on the rope.

TEACHING TIPS: Breaking this effect down into small component parts and practicing each part separately will make it easier to learn. More supple rope will work best.

THERAPEUTIC CONSIDERATIONS: This effect requires a great deal of bilateral fine motor control.

Coin through Handkerchief ***

WHAT THE AUDIENCE SEES: Performer displays a quarter between his left thumb and index finger. He drapes a handkerchief over the left hand, and the quarter penetrates the handkerchief without making a hole in it.

PROPS/SPECIAL PREPARATION: A coin and handkerchief.

ROUTINE:

Hold the coin between the thumb and index finger of your left hand with the fingers facing up (Figure 5-14a).

Drape the handkerchief over the coin and left hand. The coin should be at about the center of the handkerchief.

With your right hand, pretend to adjust the coin through the handkerchief, and at the same time secretly pinch a small fold of cloth between your left thumb and the coin (Figure 5-14b).

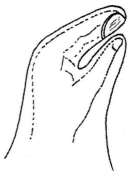

Figure 5-14a   Figure 5-14b

Now bring the front edge of the handkerchief (the edge toward the audience) toward you, folding it back on itself over your left wrist to show the audience the coin one more time.

Here is the secret move: bring both edges of the handkerchief resting on your left wrist back over the coin. The coin is now no longer inside the handkerchief.

With the right hand, grasp the handkerchief a few inches past the coin, twisting the handkerchief around the coin (Figure 5-14c).

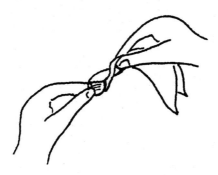

Figure 5-14c

As you twist, the coin will start to become visible. Continue twisting the handkerchief until the coin has totally "penetrated" it.

Allow the coin and handkerchief to be examined.

TEACHING TIPS: This effect is even stronger with a borrowed coin and handkerchief.

THERAPEUTIC CONSIDERATIONS: A larger coin will make this effect easier to accomplish.

Cut and Restored Rope ***

WHAT THE AUDIENCE SEES: A five-foot piece of rope is cut in the center and tied together. After a little magic, the rope is completely restored.

PROPS/SPECIAL PREPARATION: A five-foot piece of rope and a pair of scissors.

ROUTINE:

Display rope by holding the ends between your left thumb and fingers, allowing the center of the rope to hang down (Figure 5-15a).

Insert your right thumb and index finger through the loop and use them to grasp point X, which is four inches below the right end (Figure 5-15b).

Figure 5-15a   Figure 5-15b

Pull point X upward as it forms a small secret loop, which is hidden by your left hand. The actual center of the rope will slide off your fingers and onto this secret loop (Figure 5-15c).

Hold this loop with your left thumb and index finger. To the audience it looks as if you just brought the center of the rope up to the left hand. Cut the rope at point X with the scissors (Figure 5-15d). Put the scissors in your right pocket.

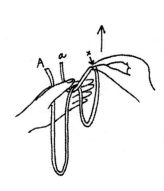

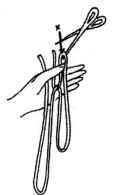

Figure 5-15c   Figure 5-15d

The audience will see four ends of rope. Let the ends of the rope on the far right and left drop to show two "separate" pieces of rope. The loop remains hidden by your left hand.

Tie the two ends of the short loop around the center of the long piece of rope. It now looks as if you have two pieces of rope tied together. Display the rope with the knot in the center.

Wrap the rope around your left hand as you secretly slide the knot off into your right hand. Reach your right hand into your pocket to get the scissors and leave the knot in the pocket. Use the scissors as a magic wand to wave over the left hand, then show the rope fully restored.

TEACHING TIPS: For a comical ending, the knot can be visibly slid of the rope and tossed to someone in the audience.

THERAPEUTIC CONSIDERATIONS: Individuals who have difficulty using scissors may ask a spectator to cut the rope.

6 | Mind Bending Magic

Crayon Telepathy *

WHAT THE AUDIENCE SEES: A spectator selects a crayon while the performer's back is turned. The selected crayon is placed in the performer's hand behind her back. Without looking at the crayon, the performer correctly identifies the color of the selected crayon.

PROPS/SPECIAL PREPARATION: Four crayons of different colors; primary colors work best.

ROUTINE:

Explain that you will attempt to read the spectator's mind. Have the spectator mentally select one of the crayons, then turn your back and have the spectator place the selected crayon in your hand.

Turn and face the spectator and ask him to concentrate on the color. As you are facing the spectator, color one of your thumbnails with the crayon.

Turn your back to the spectator again and have him take the crayon and place it with the others. Make sure the spectator doesn't see your colored thumbnail.

Face the spectator and raise your hands to eye level, with your palms facing him. Make a magical gesture, as if you are trying to read his mind. As you do this, look at your thumb and see what color is on your thumbnail.

Pause, as if concentrating, and then announce his selected color.

TEACHING TIPS: Don't make it obvious that you are looking at your thumbnail.

THERAPEUTIC CONSIDERATIONS: This is an excellent effect to practice fine motor skills without visual input (coloring the thumbnail behind the back).

Think of a Number **

WHAT THE AUDIENCE SEES: Performer has a spectator write down a number with three different digits. The spectator performs some simple computations with her number. Amazingly, her calculated number matches the performer's prediction.

PROPS/SPECIAL PREPARATION: Paper and a pencil. On another piece of paper write the number 1089 and fold it to conceal the number.

ROUTINE:

Display your previously prepared folded piece of paper. Ask a spectator to write down a three-digit number, making sure all three digits are different.

Have the spectator reverse her number (Figure 6-1a). If this reversed number is larger than the original number, she is to write the number above her number. If the reversed number is less than the original number, she is to write the number below her number.

Have her subtract the numbers. The remainder must be a three digit number, so if it is a two digit number (such as "99" as in Figure 6-1b), she must put a zero before the two digit number (Figure 6-1b).

Tell her to reverse the digits of her answer.

Add these reversed digits to the previous remainder (Figure 6-1c). The answer is always 1089. Have the spectator open your folded piece of paper to reveal your prediction.

$$342$$
$$243$$

$$\begin{array}{r} 342 \\ -\ 243 \\ \hline 099 \end{array}$$

Figure 6-1a   Figure 6-1b

$$\begin{array}{r} 099 \\ +\ 990 \\ \hline 1089 \end{array}$$

Figure 6-1c

TEACHING TIPS: If necessary, a calculator can be used.

THERAPEUTIC CONSIDERATIONS: Have the student use different fingers on a calculator for isolated motor control.

Number prediction **

WHAT THE AUDIENCE SEES: Ask a spectator to think of any number. After a few calculations, the performer tells the spectator what number she initially chose.

PROPS/SPECIAL PREPARATION: A calculator if necessary.

ROUTINE:

Have a spectator think of any number.

Once the number is selected, have her multiply her number by two, then add 12, divide by two, and subtract the originally chosen number. The answer will always be six.

TEACHING TIPS: Choosing a small number should allow the calculations to be made without the use of a calculator.

THERAPEUTIC CONSIDERATIONS: The student may use small objects, such as pennies or marbles, to actually perform the calculations. Each counted object can be deliberately picked up and put in a container.

Calculated Birth Date **

WHAT THE AUDIENCE SEES: With the use of a calculator, the spectator performs a number of calculations. The answer is the spectator's birth date.

PROPS/SPECIAL PREPARATION: A calculator.

ROUTINE: This effect is self-working. Have the spectator follow these steps exactly:

Enter the number of the month he was born

Multiply by 4

Add 13

Multiply by 25

Subtract 200

Add the day of the month he was born

Multiply by 2

Subtract 40

Multiply by 50

Add the last two digits of the year he was born

Subtract 10,500

The answer is always the spectator's birth date.

TEACHING TIPS: Proceed carefully with each calculation.

THERAPEUTIC CONSIDERATIONS: This effect is excellent for integration of following directions, using math concepts, and fine motor control using a calculator.

Elephant from Denmark ***

WHAT THE AUDIENCE SEES: The performer asks any number of spectators to think of a number, a country, an animal and a color. The performer tells the spectators exactly what they are thinking.

PROPS/SPECIAL PREPARATION: none.

ROUTINE: This effect almost works itself. Have the spectator(s) follow these directions:

Think of any number from one to ten.

Multiply that number by 9.

If it is a two-digit number, add them together.

Subtract five from that number. Use that number and correspond it to a letter of the alphabet. For example, if you were thinking of number one, it would correspond to letter "A". Number two would correspond to letter " B" and so on.

Now think of a country that begins with that letter.

Think of the second letter of that country.

Using the second letter of the country, think of an animal that begins with that letter.

Lastly, think of the color of that animal.

Ask how many of the spectators are thinking of a gray elephant in Denmark (most people will).

TEACHING TIPS: This effect is more amazing when performed for a large audience.

THERAPEUTIC CONSIDERATIONS: You may want to have the student read the directions until he is able to memorize them.

7 | Fantastic Fun

Mushroom President *

WHAT THE AUDIENCE SEES: The performer folds a dollar bill, turning George Washington into a giant mushroom.

PROPS/SPECIAL PREPARATION: A real dollar bill.

ROUTINE:

Crease the dollar bill just above George's eyebrows as shown (fold "A" in Figure 7-1a).

Bring fold "A" toward you, to just below George's chin (Figure 7-1b).

Figure 7-1a   Figure 7-1b

TEACHING TIPS: A crisp dollar bill works best.

THERAPEUTIC CONSIDERATIONS: The creasing of the bill will enhance pinch grip.

Walking Through a Piece of Paper **

WHAT THE AUDIENCE SEES: The performer states that he can cut a hole in a piece of construction paper and walk through the hole. He makes a number of cuts in the paper. He slowly unfolds the paper and steps through it.

PROPS/SPECIAL PREPARATION: An 8 ½ x 11-inch piece of construction paper and scissors.

ROUTINE:

Fold the paper in half lengthwise.

Using the scissors, make cuts as shown in Figure 7-2a.

Unfold the paper and cut from point X to Y (Figure 7-2b). Open the paper into a large circle and step through it.

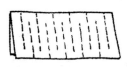

Figure 7-2a

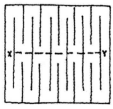

Figure 7-2b

TEACHING TIPS: Leave an uncut border of at least one inch at the edges of the paper. The more cuts made (as in Figure 7-2a), the larger the circle will be. Experiment with smaller sizes of paper.

THERAPEUTIC CONSIDERATIONS: This effect enhances not only fine motor control of the hands, but also single leg standing balance as the student lifts up one foot, then the other, to step through the circle.

Fortuneteller ***

This paper folding technique was originally used to provide simple fortunes. As you will see, it can be applied to a variety of other uses.

PROPS/SPECIAL PREPARATION: A piece of paper approximately eight inches square and a pen. Fold the paper in half and in half again. Open and the paper appears as in Figure 7-3a. Fold each corner to the center point (Figure 7-3b).

 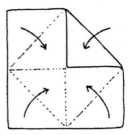

Figure 7-3a   Figure 7-3b

Now your paper appears as in Figure 7-3c. Turn the folded paper face down, and fold each corner to the center again (Figure 7-3d).

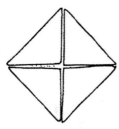 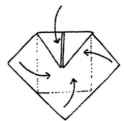

Figure 7-3c   Figure 7-3d

Now your paper appears as in Figure 7-3e. Fold the top half of the folded paper toward you, over the bottom half (Figure 7-3f).

 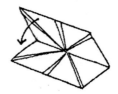

Figure 7-3e   Figure 7-3f

Now your paper looks like Figure 7-3g. There are four flaps at the top. Turn the folded paper upside down, so the flaps are at the bottom, and put your left thumb and index finger under the left flaps (Figure 7-3h) and your right thumb and index finger under the right flaps. Bring your thumbs and index fingers together at the center. Now the fortuneteller can be opened in two different directions.

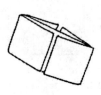

Figure 7-3g

Figure 7-3h

Number the four flaps as shown (Figure 7-3i).

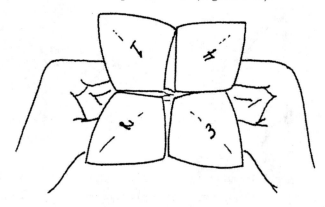

Figure 7-3i

When you open the fortuneteller one way, there are four triangles; when you open it the other way, there are four different triangles. Number these one through eight. Inside the fortuneteller you will now have four flaps, each with two numbers on it. Lift up each flap and write a "fortune" underneath (or write two fortunes, one on each half of the flap).

ROUTINE:

Ask the spectator to choose a number from one through four, as shown in Figure 7-3i.

Open the fortuneteller alternately in each direction that number of times. Then ask the spectator to choose another number visible inside the fortuneteller. Open the fortuneteller alternately in each direction that number of times.

Ask the spectator to choose another number from those visible inside, and lift the flap on which that number is written. His fortune appears inside.

TEACHING TIPS: Students may write their own "fortunes" or other messages, jokes, etc.

THERAPEUTIC CONSIDERATIONS: A speech therapy application would be to write specific words that challenge the student rather than numbers on the flaps. Rather than counting, the students could spell those words. Alternately, stickers with different colors or pictures can be used on the flaps. The fortuneteller can also be useful for home exercise programs. Students can use the fortuneteller to select the exercises written by the therapist on the inside flaps. This would provide variety and more fun to the student's exercise program. In a classroom setting, the fortuneteller can be used to practice vocabulary words.

Napkin Rose ***

WHAT THE AUDIENCE SEES: Performer folds a cocktail size napkin into a rose.

PROPS/SPECIAL PREPARATION: A cocktail napkin, red if possible. If you have a three-ply napkin, carefully separate each layer. The rose will look better if you use a one-ply napkin.

ROUTINE:

Grip the unfolded napkin between the index and middle fingers of the left hand (Figure 7-4a).

Keeping the napkin there, wrap it around both fingers (Figure 7-4b) until you form a tube.

 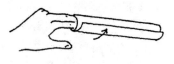

Figure 7-4a   Figure 7-4b

Pinch the napkin with the right thumb and index finger and begin twisting as in Figure 7-4c. Continue twisting until you are about three inches from the bottom.

Find a corner at the bottom and carefully bring it up along the stem; this will form the leaf (Figure 7-4d).

 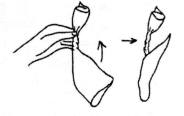

Figure 7-4c   Figure 7-4d

Continue twisting below the leaf until finished (Figure 7-4e).

Figure 7-4e

To complete the bowl of the flower, reach inside the bowl with the thumb and index finger and grasp a corner.

Adjust or twist this corner until it forms a spiral.

TEACHING TIPS: This requires a fair amount of practice to make the rose correctly.

THERAPEUTIC CONSIDERATIONS: This activity may require more one-on-one assistance than many of the other effects in this book.

Scarf Juggling
One scarf*/ Two scarves**

This is an easy type of juggling, since it happens in slow motion and can be performed with one or two scarves.

PROPS/SPECIAL PREPARATION: One or two scarves. Fourteen-inch square scarves of different colors work best.

ONE SCARF ROUTINE:

Hold the scarf by its center with your right hand. Bring your right arm up and across your body to the left as you release the scarf, keeping your palm facing away from you (Figure 7-5a).

Reach up with the left hand and catch the scarf, bringing it straight down to your left side (Figure 7-5b).

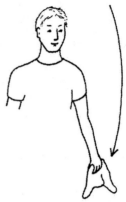

Figure 7-5a   Figure 7-5b

Repeat the same movement with the left hand by reaching across your body to the right and releasing the scarf.

Continue alternating with your right and left arms creating a figure eight pattern (Figure 7-5c).

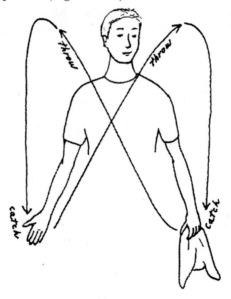

Figure 7-5c

TWO SCARF ROUTINE:

Hold a scarf by its center with each hand. Toss the scarf in your right hand as above.

Immediately toss the scarf in your left hand as above. (The path of the scarves should make an "X" in front of your chest).

Catch the first scarf with your left hand, bringing it straight down, and then catch the second scarf with your right hand.

TEACHING TIPS: Using music with a strong beat will help keep the juggling rhythm easier. Try to keep exceeding your best number of tosses without an error.

THERAPEUTIC CONSIDERATIONS: An easier starting point would be for the student to pass the scarf from hand to hand around his head, neck, chest, hips, between his legs, etc. This could also be accomplished with a partner. Use of one scarf provides an opportunity to cross the midline and incorporates significant eye-hand coordination. Tossing the scarves higher can increase shoulder range of motion. Changing the base of support (for example, sitting, kneeling, standing on both legs, or standing on one leg) can vary the difficulty level of this effect. Once the juggling motor pattern becomes fairly automatic, have the student recite a poem or sing a song while juggling.

8 | Magic That Tells A Story

Telling a story or making your point utilizing a magic effect can make your message more memorable. For example, a teacher or therapist may perform one of the following effects to introduce the concept of using magic as a motor skill activity. These magic effects can also be used to illustrate a key point in public speaking. Often it is more difficult devising a story to accompany your magic than learning the steps to the effect itself. The following pieces of magic can be used to tell a variety of stories.

Equal, Unequal Ropes ***

WHAT THE AUDIENCE SEES: Three pieces of rope of different lengths become the same length.

PROPS/SPECIAL PREPARATION: you need three pieces of soft rope, 36, 24 and 10 inches in length.

ROUTINE:

Display each rope separately. Your left palm will face you throughout this routine. As you show each rope, place the long rope into the thumb web space of the left hand. The medium length rope is placed alongside it and the short rope is placed next to that. Two to three inches of rope should hang over the top of the left hand (Figure 8-1a).

The right hand now brings up the bottom end of the long piece and places it between the top ends of the medium and short pieces (Figure 8-1b).

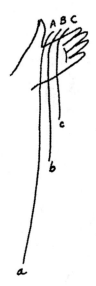

Figure 8-1a   Figure 8-1b

Next bring up the bottom end of the medium piece and place it to the right side of the short piece (Figure 8-1c).

Reach your right hand through the loop formed by the long piece, and grasp the bottom end of the short piece, placing it to the right of its top end (Figure 8-1d). It looks to the audience as if you have shown three pieces of rope and brought the bottom ends into the hand. Meanwhile, your left hand conceals the loop of the short rope around the long rope.

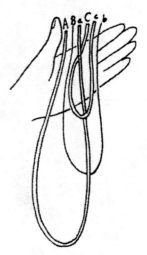

Figure 8-1c   Figure 8-1d

You make the ropes appear to be equal in length as follows: the right hand pulls ends C, c, b to the right, while the remaining ends (A, B, a) remain held in the left hand. The secret loop remains hidden by the right hand (Figure 8-1e).

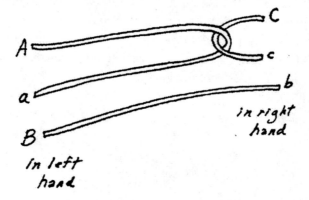

Figure 8-1e

To convince the audience that you indeed have three equal lengths of rope, you need to show them separately as you count them. First transfer the ropes to the left hand, concealing the secret loop. To count the ropes, the right hand takes the top end of the medium rope (Bb) between its index and middle fingers from the left hand and pulls it to the right as you count "one," letting the bottom end drop free.

The right hand now puts the medium rope between the left index and middle fingers. At the same time, the right index finger and thumb grasp the short and long ropes as a unit (still concealing the secret loop) and pull them to the right as you count "two," again letting the end drop.

Count "three" by pulling the medium rope again from the left hand, and letting the end drop. The audience will think you have displayed three pieces of rope of the same length.

To return the ropes to their original length, put the ropes back in the left hand with the medium rope in the thumb web space and the looped ropes to the right of it. Bring up one end of the long rope and place it to the far right of the ends you are holding. Bring up the other end of the long rope and place it to the far left. Bring up the end of the medium rope and place it to the far right.

Now keep hold of the three left most ends with the left thumb and index finger, as you drop the three ends on the right. It will appear that all the ropes have returned to their original lengths.

Story ideas:

- Although people appear different, they are all really the same.
- There are many ways of accomplishing a goal, but the result is the same.
- Use your imagination and pretend these three pieces of rope are pieces of spaghetti or taffy.

Dental Floss Miracle **

WHAT THE AUDIENCE SEES: The performer cuts several pieces of floss from a box of dental floss. All but one piece of floss is rolled into a small bundle. The bundle is squeezed onto the remaining piece of floss. The ends of the strand are pulled and the pieces unravel into one long restored length of dental floss.

PROPS/SPECIAL PREPARATION: one box of waxed dental floss. Hold the open box of floss in the left hand with the side with the writing facing you. With the right hand, pull out about eighteen inches of floss and drape it over the left index finger. Wrap this piece of floss around the left index and middle fingers, leaving about three inches at the end hanging free. Remove the loop with the right hand and give it a gentle squeeze to form it into a circle. Gently twist the loop into a figure 8 and press the two small loops of the figure 8 together into one small circle. Squeeze the small circle of floss to form a bundle, then fold it in half and use the remaining three inches of floss to loop around the bundle three times. You should have about a two-inch tail coming from the bundle. Place the end of the tail under the metal cutter in the box and the bundle in the trough of the box. Close the lid.

ROUTINE:

Hold the box of floss in the left hand between the index and middle fingers. Open the box with your right hand, the writing side of the box facing you. Secretly grasp the hidden bundle of floss with the right thumb and index finger, and tear a three to four inch piece of floss from the box. Place this piece of floss between the left thumb and index finger, concealing the secret bundle.

The ends of the floss project above and below the left fingers. With the right hand, tear off another piece of floss and place it next to the first piece in the left hand. Repeat four to five more times. Close the box with the right hand and put it down.

With the right fingers, pull the loose strands up, leaving the piece with the bundle behind. This will be easy because the bundle will be anchored between the left fingers. Roll the loose pieces between the right thumb and index finger until you have a bundle the same size as the one attached to the piece in your left hand.

Place the bundle in the right hand next to the bundle in your left hand. At this time show your right hand empty. Pretend to roll the bundle and strand together between your left thumb and index finger. Now transfer both bundles of floss to your right thumb and index finger. Show your left hand empty.

The strand with the bundle should be to the left of the bundle of separate pieces of floss. At this point, the only thing the audience sees are two ends of floss extending above and below your right thumb and index finger. The left thumb and index finger grasp one end of the strand, as your right thumb and index finger grasp the other end.

Show the strand of floss with the secret bundle attached. Slowly pull the ends apart to show it restored.

Pick up the box of floss with your right hand and put it along with the bundle of separate pieces of floss in your pocket.

Story ideas:
- Everyone makes mistakes. The important thing is that you learn from your mistakes.
- There are many parts to solving a problem.
- Teamwork can accomplish anything.

Cut & Restored Rope ***

WHAT THE AUDIENCE SEES: A five-foot piece of rope is cut in the center and tied together. After a little magic, the rope is completely restored.

PROPS/SPECIAL PREPARATION: A five-foot piece of rope and a pair of scissors.

ROUTINE: refer to chapter 5.

Story ideas:

Mistakes (cutting the rope) are correctable.

Things usually work out for the best.

Thumb Tip **

This useful utility prop can be used to vanish a paper napkin, vanish salt, change two dimes and a nickel for a quarter, restore a torn bill, or link paper clips together. Thumb tips can be purchased at any magic shop for about $3.00.

Key points regarding thumb tips:

When you wear the thumb tip, do not slide it over the knuckle.

If the thumb tip is too large, wrap masking tape around the inside of the tip to make it fit more snugly.

Don't worry how the thumb tip looks; with proper technique no one will notice it.

Do not stick your thumb with the thumb tip straight up in the air (palm facing audience).

Use the hand wearing the thumb tip naturally, but try to keep the tip facing directly toward the audience when it is fully exposed. This makes it difficult to see.

Try to keep the hand wearing the thumb tip moving.

Vanishing napkin

Place the thumb tip in your left hand before you perform this effect. Curl your fingers loosely around the thumb tip. Hold the napkin in your right hand. Let your left hand hang relaxed at your side.

Display the napkin with your right hand, then make a fist with your left hand. Slowly tuck the napkin into your left hand (thumb tip). Continue pushing the napkin into your fist until it is almost completely into the thumb tip. Push the remaining bit of napkin into your fist with your right thumb.

Secretly steal out the thumb tip on your right thumb as your right hand moves away. In other words, your right thumb is wearing the thumb tip.

Show your left hand empty. Gently brush your hands together (keeping the right thumb pointing directly toward the audience). This will subtly show both hands empty.

To reproduce the napkin, bend your thumb (with the thumb

tip) into the palm of your hand. Remove your thumb from the thumb tip, and reach into the fist with your left hand and remove the napkin.

Vanishing salt

Start with the thumb tip in your left hand.

Take the lid off a salt shaker and slowly pour some salt into your left fist (thumb tip) until the thumb tip is about half full.

Act as if you are brushing some salt off the top of your left hand and secretly steal away the thumb tip with your right thumb.

Show that the salt has vanished from your left hand.

Bend your right thumb down into your fist to remove the thumb tip and slowly pour the salt out of the right hand into a cup.

Change for a quarter

The thumb tip and a quarter are palmed in the left hand. Borrow two dimes and a nickel.

Slowly push the two dimes and nickel into the left fist (thumb tip).

As you push the last coin into your fist, steal out the thumb tip.

Open your hand and reveal the quarter.

Torn and restored bill

You will need two one-dollar bills in identical condition. Palm the thumb tip and one of the bills folded in your left hand.

Tear the second dollar bill into four pieces and place them into the left fist (thumb tip).

As you place the last piece into the fist, steal out the thumb tip.

Open your hand and reveal the restored bill.

Linking paper clips

Palm 12 linked paper clips and a thumb tip in your left hand.

Push 12 unlinked paper clips into your left fist (thumb tip).

When you push the last paper clip into your fist, steal out the thumb tip on your right thumb.

Open your left hand and show the paper clips linked.

Sponge Balls or Stars **

Sponge balls or stars are one of the best ways to learn basic sleight of hand magic. They can be purchased in a set of four at any magic shop. Use either the one and one-half or two-inch size sponge ball. The use of sponge stars rather than balls can provide more story ideas, in that they are more unique. This is a great effect because it happens in the spectator's hands.

WHAT THE AUDIENCE SEES: A sponge ball disappears from the performer's hand and appears in the spectator's hand.

PROPS/SPECIAL PREPARATION: two to four sponge balls.

ROUTINE:

Begin with two sponge balls on the table. Pick up one of them with the right hand and, performing the finger palm vanish as described in Chapter 3, pretend to place it in the left hand. (The sponge ball is concealed in the right curled ring and little fingers.) To the spectator it should look as if you simply picked up one of the balls and placed it in your left hand.

Immediately pick up the second ball with your right hand (which secretly contains the first ball), and display it between your thumb and index finger.

Ask the spectator to hold out one of his hands, palm up. Place both sponge balls in his hand and help him close his hand quickly, preventing the two balls from separating. Because the balls are made of sponge, the spectator will be unable to determine that he is holding two balls instead of one.

Count to three and slowly open your left hand to show that the ball has vanished. The spectator will be amazed to find the two balls in his hand. This effect can be developed further by using three or four sponge balls and having an increasing number of balls appear in the spectator's hand. For instance, you could casually reach into your right pocket and finger palm another ball when the spectator opens his hand to find the two balls. Pick up both of those balls with your right hand and place them (and the extra hidden ball) into another spectator's hand. That spectator will now find three balls when he opens his hand.

Story ideas:
- One good idea leads to another.
- Everyone has magic within him.

Cut and Restored Newspaper *

WHAT THE AUDIENCE SEES: A piece of newspaper is cut and is instantly restored. This can be repeated a number of times with the same result.

PROPS/SPECIAL PREPARATION: A piece of newspaper, rubber cement, scissors, and flour or talcum powder.

Preparation: Cut a three inch wide and twenty to twenty-two inch long strip of newspaper and fold it in half. Open the strip of newspaper and lay it flat. On the inside of the newspaper apply a two to three inch wide area of rubber cement on either side of the fold and allow it to dry (Figure 8-2a). Keep the paper open so the glued areas don't touch. Apply another layer of rubber cement and allow it to dry. Sprinkle talcum powder or flour over the rubber cement.

ROUTINE:

Display the strip of newspaper. Fold it in half at the natural fold of the newspaper with the glued portion inside the fold.

Cut the newspaper about 3/4 of an inch below the fold (Figure 8-2b).

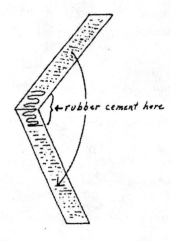

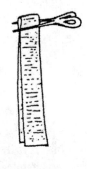

Figure 8-2a   Figure 8-2b

Take one end of the strip and let the other end fall. It will appear as if you still have one whole strip of newspaper. The glued area will create the appearance of the natural fold.

This can be repeated a number of times based on how far you applied the glue to each side of the fold. You can also cut the paper on an angle and it will appear restored.

Story ideas:

- First impressions may not always be accurate.
- Some things aren't as easy as they look.
- Persistence pays off (it may take multiple cuts until the paper is actually cut in two pieces).

9 | Final Thoughts

As you probably already know, practice makes permanent. Practicing a few minutes a day will produce the best results. I think it is much better to perform two or three magic effects well, than to perform a dozen poorly. The key to entertaining magic is the ability to incorporate your personal experiences, beliefs or passions into the presentations.

If you perform long enough, you'll encounter two of the most common audience problems. What about the spectator who loudly proclaims, "I know how you did that"? Personally I handle this situation in one of two ways. I either totally ignore the comments, or I congratulate him and ask if we can keep it as "our secret."

The other common situation is when a spectator begs you to explain how the effect was accomplished. There are many comebacks; most of which I feel are rather rude. I prefer to tell the inquisitive spectator, "If I knew how it works, I would tell you." This answer works very well, but you have to sound sincere.

I hope this book has peaked your interest in magic. There are a number of ways to continue your magical education. First, I suggest you watch other magicians perform. Television specials, festivals, stage shows and, if possible, a restaurant with a close-up magician, are all outstanding ways to learn about the performance of magic. Pay attention to the story that accompanies each effect, how the magician involves the audience, the way effects are sequenced or routined together, the naturalness of each movement, and how the magician creates a "sense of wonder" for the spectators. Secondly, many park districts offer magic classes. Another idea is to purchase some of the books in the bibliography or one of the hundreds of magic videos available. I'd recommend visiting a magic shop to ask which videos are worth purchasing. You may also wish to subscribe to a magic magazine or join one of the international magic organizations, such as the International Brotherhood of Magicians or the Society of American Magicians. There are local chapters of these organizations in hundreds of towns across the country. Of course, you can always contact me at my email address (appliedmagic@earthlink.net). I will help you anyway I am able.

IF YOU'D LIKE TO SEE WHAT THE MAGIC EFFECTS IN THIS BOOK LOOK LIKE WHEN PERFORMED PROPERLY, ORDER A PERFORMANCE VIDEO BY CALLING (630) 717-8537.

Magic Magazines:
Magic, THE INDEPENDENT MAGAZINE FOR MAGICIANS (702) 798-4893
Genii, THE INTERNATIONAL CONJUROR'S MAGAZINE (213) 935-2848

Magic Organizations:
International Brotherhood of Magicians (315) 845-9200 (www.magician.org)
Society of American Magicians (314) 846-5659 (www.uelectric.com/sam/)

Bibliography

The magic effects in this book can be found in various versions in the following references:

Cassidy, John. *THE KLUTZ BOOK OF MAGIC*. Klutz Press, Palo Alto, CA. 1990.

Copperfield, David. *PROJECT MAGIC*. 1981.

Dean, Bryan. Magic and Illusion Website. Online. Available: http://www.magic.about.com/hobbies/magic

Eldon, Peter. *THE MAGIC HANDBOOK*. Simon & Schuster, New York. 1985.

Finnigan, Dave. *THE JOY OF JUGGLING BOOK*. Jugglebug, Inc. Edmonds, Washington. 1993.

Fulves, Karl. *EASY MAGIC*. Dover Publications, New York. 1995.

Gardner, Martin. *MARTIN GARDNER'S TABLE MAGIC*. Dover Publications, Mineola, New York. 1998.

Pogue, David. *MAGIC FOR DUMMIES*. IDG Books Worldwide Inc, Foster City, CA. 1998.

Robbins, D. *102 E-Z MAGIC TRICKS*. 1976.

Severn, Bill. *THE BIG BOOK OF MAGIC*. D. Mckay Co, New York. 1973.

Tarr, Bill. *NOW YOU SEE IT, NOW YOU DON'T*. Random House, New York. 1976.

Tremain, Jon. *THE AMAZING BOOK OF MAGIC AND CARD TRICKS*. Quadrillion Publishing Ltd., New York. 1996

Wilson, Mark. *MARK WILSON'S COMPLETE COURSE IN MAGIC*. Ottenheimer Publishers, Philadelphia. 1988.

Index